All About Reptiles

ACTIVITY BOOK

by Debra Chana Mostow
Illustrations by Manny Campana

SCHOLASTIC INC.
New York Toronto London Auckland Sydney

ISBN 0-590-48722-1

Copyright © 1994 by Scholastic Inc.
All rights reserved. Published by Scholastic Inc.

12 11 10 9 8 7 6 5 4 3   4 5 6 7 8 9/9

Printed in the U.S.A. .   14

First Scholastic printing, September 1994

You can check your answers to the puzzles in this book on pages 31 and 32.

So Many Reptiles!

Crocodiles, alligators, lizards, snakes, and turtles are all reptiles. Reptiles have backbones, lungs, and scales, and are cold-blooded. Most reptiles live in warm places.

Find the words CROCODILE, ALLIGATOR, LIZARD, SNAKE, and TURTLE. You can look forwards, backwards, up, and down. Circle each word as you find it.

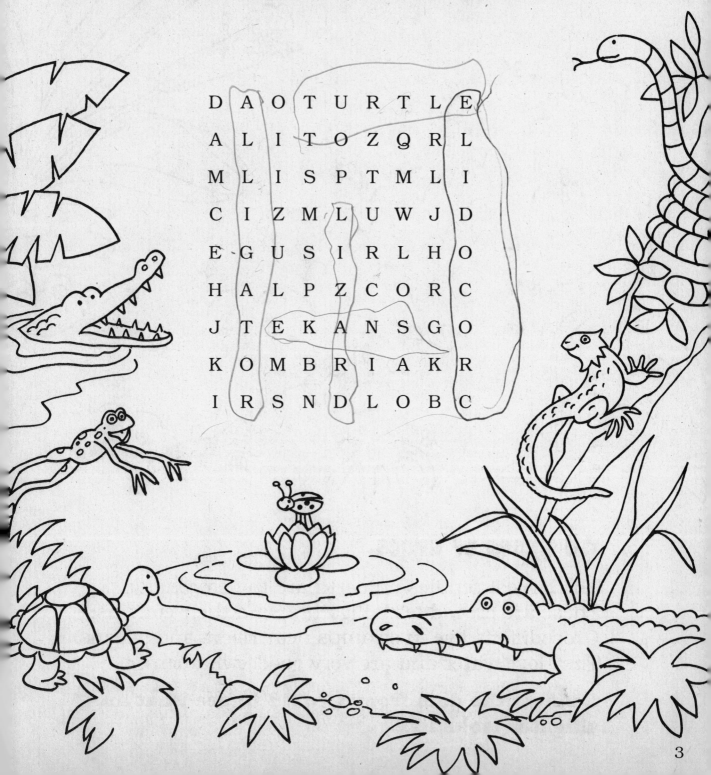

```
D A O T U R T L E
A L I T O Z Q R L
M L I S P T M L I
C I Z M L U W J D
E G U S I R L H O
H A L P Z C O R C
J T E K A N S G O
K O M B R I A K R
I R S N D L O B C
```

START

All Types of Crocs

The largest reptiles on earth are the *crocodilians*.
These are crocodiles, alligators, and their cousins.
Crocodilians live in swamps near rivers and oceans.
They love water and are very good swimmers.

Connect the dots from 1 to 38 to see what an alligator looks like.

Crocodile Rock

Most reptiles are very silent. Some have no voices at all. But one of the loudest sounds in the animal kingdom is the great roar of a large crocodile. It is known as the "song of the crocodilian."

Three of these crocodiles look exactly alike. Can you find and circle them?

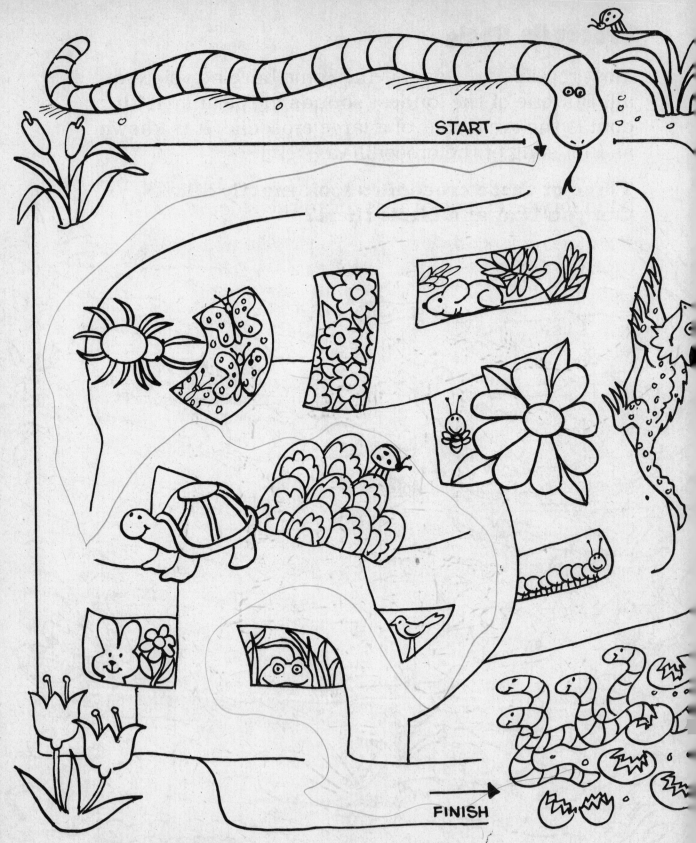

START

FINISH

Wee Reptiles

Baby reptiles hatch from eggs. Baby snakes and lizards open their shells with an egg tooth that is attached to the tip of their snouts.

Can you help this mother snake find her babies?

The Shell Game

The turtle is the only kind of reptile who carries its house on its back. When an enemy is near, the turtle just pulls its legs, head, and tail into its shell for protection. This shell helps to keep a turtle safe, but also makes it difficult to move around. A turtle cannot bend forwards, backwards, or to the side.

How many turtles can you find hidden in this picture? Circle each one as you find it.

Big and Ugly

Did you know that turtles don't have teeth? They have beaks that they use to catch their food and tear it apart. One kind of turtle has a very sharp beak and very sharp jaws that snap. This turtle can grow to be more than 200 pounds. It lives on the bottom of muddy rivers. Most turtles are gentle, but not this one.

Use this code to find out the name of this big, mean, and ugly turtle. 1 = A, 2 = B, 3 = C, and so on. The first letter is already done for you.

Code:

1	2	3	4	5	6	7	8	9	10	11	12	13
A	B	C	D	E	F	G	H	I	J	K	L	M

14	15	16	17	18	19	20	21	22	23	24	25	26
N	O	P	Q	R	S	T	U	V	W	X	Y	Z

A _ _ _ _ _ _ _ _   _ _ _ _ _ _ _ _
1 12 12 9 7 1 20 15 18   19 14 1 16 16 5 18

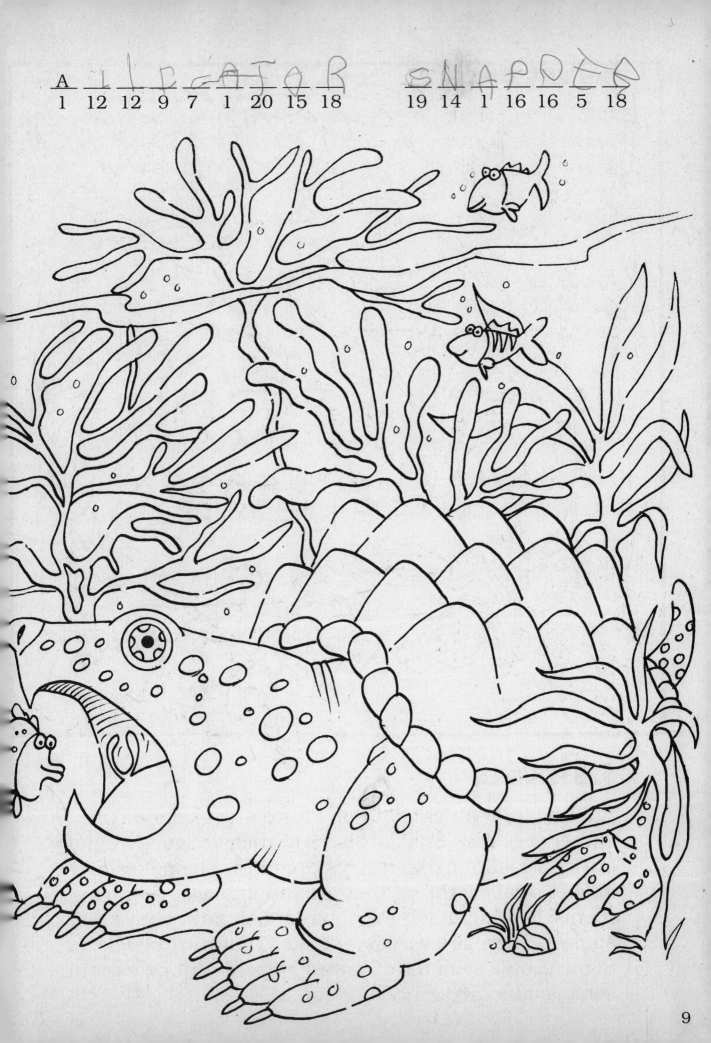

SSSSSnakes

Snakes are reptiles that don't have any legs, but can slither very fast. Snakes also run their tongues in and out very fast to make the SSSS sound. All snakes are able to swallow things that are much bigger than themselves including mice, birds, fish, and even other snakes. There are very few snakes that hurt people. Some people even have snakes as pets. But be careful, some snakes are very dangerous.

The scenes on these two pages are not alike. Circle the six things in the second scene that are different.

Rattle Alert

There are a few snakes that are poisonous and, therefore, very dangerous. These poisonous snakes bite with long, hollow teeth. The poison, called *venom*, runs through the snake's teeth. All rattlesnakes are poisonous. The rattlesnake has a rattle on its tail, which it uses when angry or frightened.

Here's how to find out the name of the long and hollow teeth that carry the snake's venom. Read each clue. When you figure out the word, write its letters in the boxes next to the number that matches the clue. The letters in the dark boxes will spell out the name of these poisonous teeth.

1. this keeps you cool in the summer
2. some farm animals live in this
3. the opposite of closed
4. these grow on vines
5. you catch this in your mitt

1. FAN
2. BARN
3. OPEN
4. GRAPES
5. BASEBALL

Flip-flop

The hognose snake is a gentle snake. It has no rattle or venom, and it never bites. Instead, when an enemy is near, the hognose puffs up its body and hisses loudly. If the enemy won't go away, the hognose rolls over and plays dead. If someone flips the hognose over, it flops right back.

Circle four things that do not belong in this picture.

To Toad the Truth

The horned toad looks like a toad, and often acts like a toad, but it isn't really a toad—it's a lizard. Horned toads live in the desert, and like to stay out in the hot sun and chase insects. When the sun goes down and the big animals come out to hunt, the horned toad hides in the sand.

Look at this desert scene. There are five horned toads hiding in it. Find and circle them.

14

Nest Sweet Nest

Alligators build nests for their eggs. The mother makes these nests out of wet leaves and branches that she pushes into a big pile. Then, with her back feet, she digs a hole and lays her eggs. About nine weeks later the mother alligator hears little peeping noises, which means the baby alligators are ready to hatch. She tears open the nest and helps her babies to come out.

Look at this scene very carefully. Then take the memory quiz on the next page.

How Good Is Your Memory?

Circle the picture in each scene that is exactly the same as the one on pages 16 and 17.

Splish Splash

Not all snakes live on land. Some snakes live in the water and only come to the surface when they need to breathe. These snakes eat frogs, toads, newts, and fish.

To find out the name of this water snake, cross out the letters B, D, F, and G. Write the leftover letter in each row on the lines below.

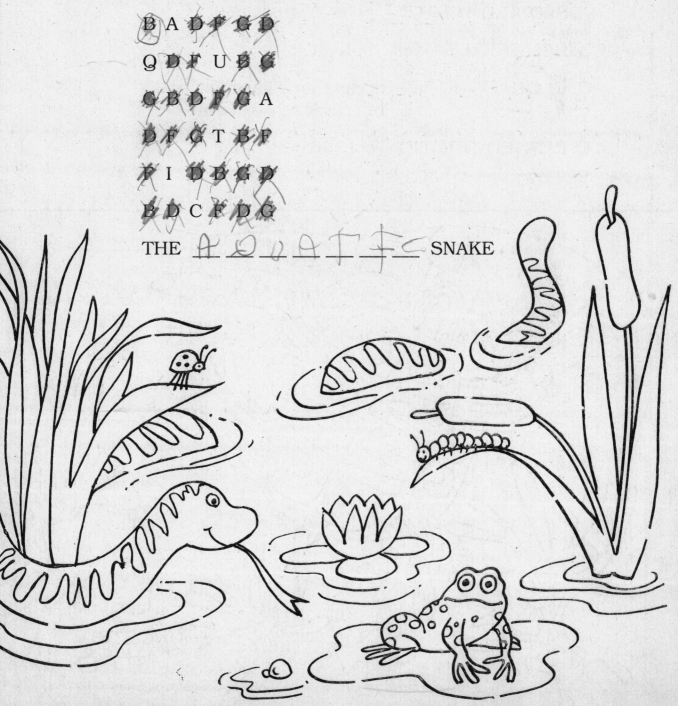

B A D F G D
Q D F U B G
G B D F G A
D F G T B F
F I D B G D
B D C F D G

THE ___A Q U A T I C___ SNAKE

The Name Game

Did you know that turtles were around at the time of the dinosaurs? And that there are about 200 different kinds of turtles. Turtles that live only on land are called tortoises.

Here are four kinds of tortoises and a picture of what each looks like. Try to match each name with the correct tortoise.

A. SPOTTED TURTLE — polka-dotted shell

B. BOX TURTLE — very high shell

C. CACTUS TURTLE — doesn't look like a cactus, but loves to eat them

D. PAINTED TURTLE — looks like its name

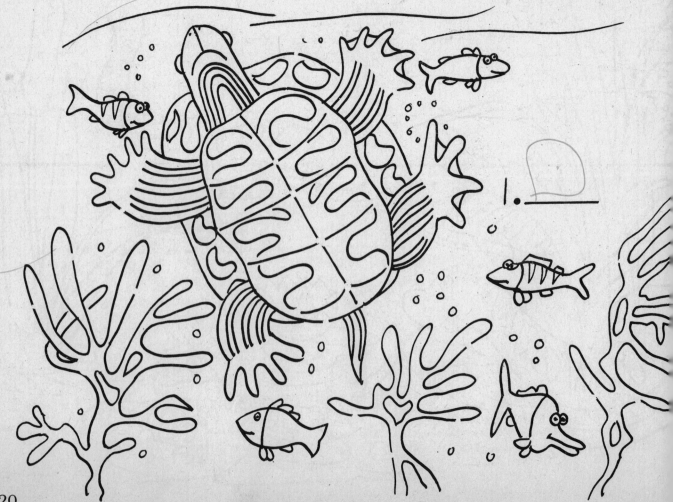

1. _____

2.

3. A

4. B

21

Tail Ends

The Gila monster is a dangerous lizard because it has venom. This lizard doesn't like the heat so it sleeps during the day. The Gila also has a very strange way of storing food. Find out what it is by solving the puzzle below.

Use the code to spell out a message about this lizard. The first letter is done for you.

W H E N   T H E   G I L A   E A T S
Z T J K   M T J   V Q H O   J O M I

A   L O T   N I S   T A I L
O   H W M   T Q I   M O Q H

G E T S   E A T .
V J M I   Y O M

A = Q   N = K
B = D   O = A
C = Z   P = Y
D = M   Q = I
E = U   R = X
F = C   S = B
G = R   T = H
H = L   U = P
I = S   V = G
J = E   W = O
K = N   X = J
L = V   Y = F
M = T   Z = W

Towering Tortoises

The biggest of all tortoises are the Galapagos tortoises. Their legs are so thick that some say they look like elephant legs. Some of these tortoises weigh more than 500 pounds!

Connect the dots from 1 to 25 to see what a Galapagos tortoise looks like.

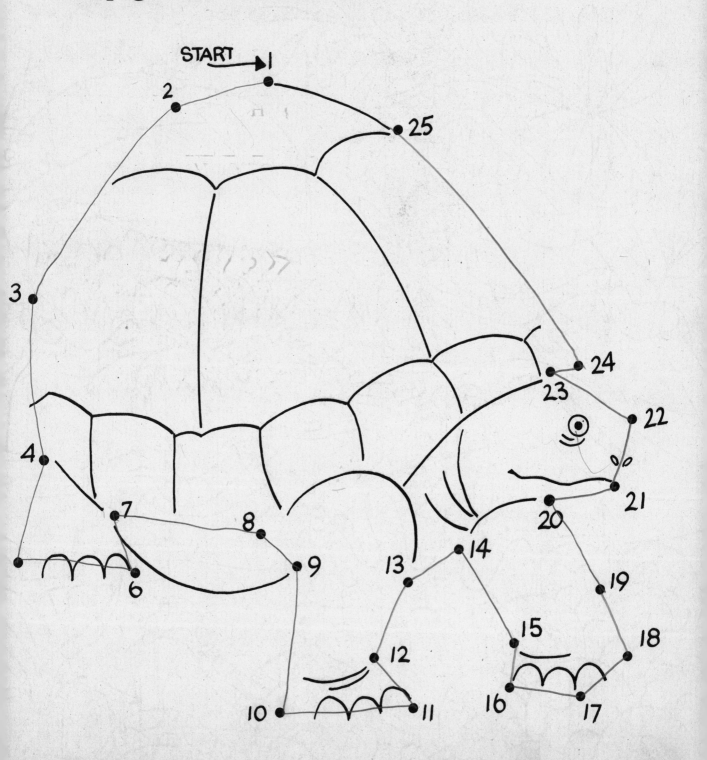

Let It All Shed Off

As a snake grows, it gets too big for its skin, so it sheds. This happens several times in a snake's life. The skin begins to loosen first around the head, and then the snake crawls out of its old covering, which turns inside out and falls off in one piece.

Color this scene any way you like.

Croc-o-gator

How can you tell the difference between an alligator and a crocodile? The most obvious difference is the teeth. The crocodile's upper and lower teeth show when its mouth is closed. When an alligator's mouth is closed, only its upper teeth show. Also, crocodiles can move faster than alligators. And their snouts are different, too.

Circle all the crocodiles you can find.
Put an X on all the alligators you can find.
Then color this scene any way you like.

Leaping Lizards!

There are almost 3,000 different kinds of lizards. Most have four legs, walk on land, and have no voices. But there is one lizard that squeaks and squeals. This noise sounds like *gecko-gecko*. That is how this lizard got its name. The gecko lizard runs around and eats roaches, mosquitoes, and many other insects. These friendly lizards live in warm countries and some even like to live in people's houses.

Can you help this friendly gecko lizard find the mosquito for dinner?

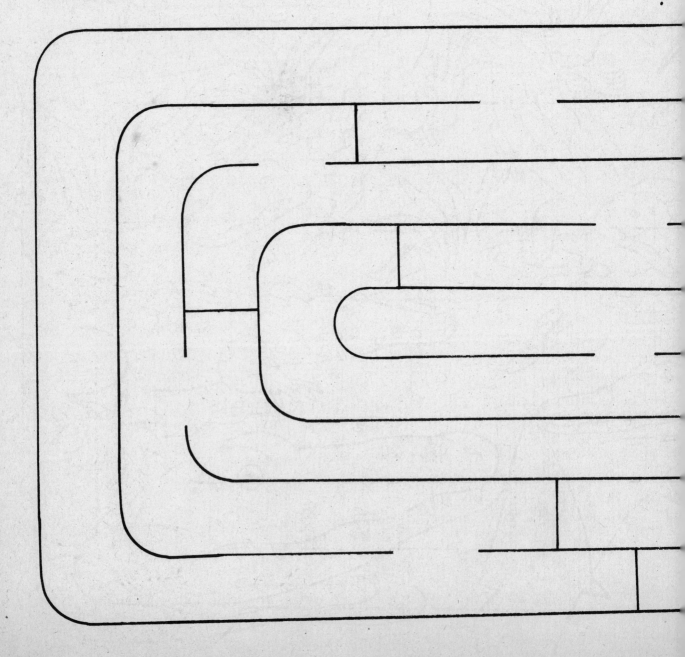

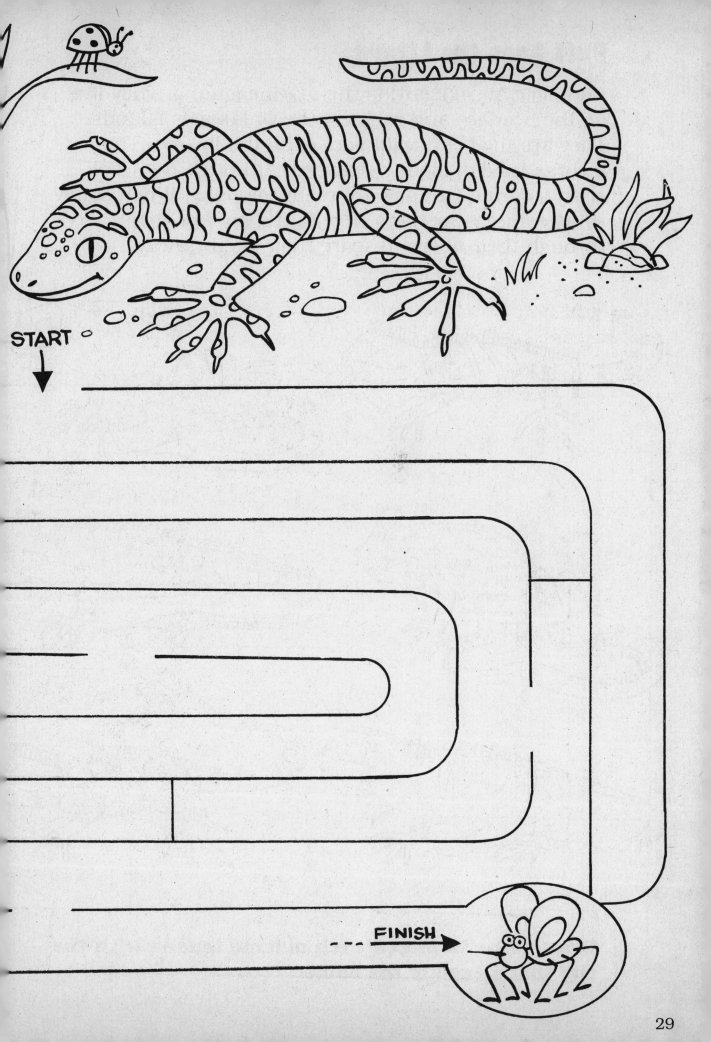

START

FINISH

29

Puff Goes the Lizard

Another type of lizard is the marine iguana. They live on the beaches and rocks of the Galapagos Islands. They are the best swimmers of all the lizards. Their favorite kind of food is seaweed. Although they look scary, marine iguanas are really very shy. When something comes near them they puff a kind of steam through their noses to scare their enemy away.

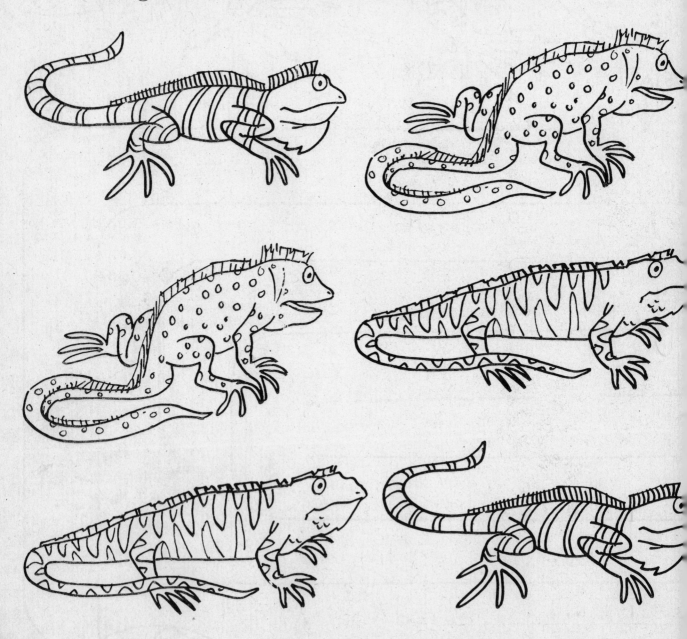

Draw a line to match each marine iguana with the one that's exactly the same.

Puzzle Answers

Page 3.
So Many Reptiles!

Page 4.
All Types of Crocs

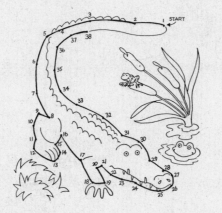

Page 5.
Crocodile Rock

Page 6. Wee Reptiles

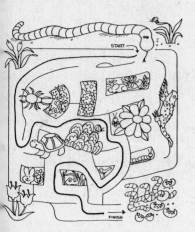

Page 7.
The Shell Game

Page 9. Big and Ugly
ALLIGATOR SNAPPER

Pages 10–11.
SSSSSnakes

Page 12. Rattle Alert

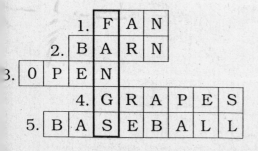

1. F A N
2. B A R N
3. O P E N
4. G R A P E S
5. B A S E B A L L

Page 13. Flip-flop

Pages 14–15. To Toad the Truth

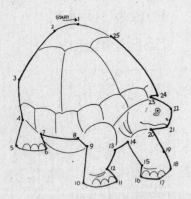

Page 19. Splish Splash
THE AQUATIC SNAKE

Page 22. Tail Ends
WHEN THE GILA EATS
A LOT HIS TAIL GETS FAT.

Page 23. Towering Tortoises

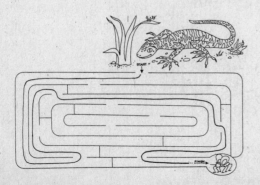

Pages 28–29. Leaping Lizards!

Page 18. How Good Is Your Memory?

Pages 20–21. The Name Game

Pages 26–27. Croc-o-gator

Page 30. Puff Goes the Lizard

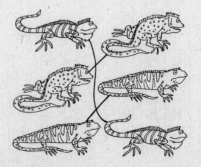